Poetry In Motion

Moving Forward To The Next Level

Poems Written By
Muletta Hayes

Cover Designed by Michela Fellows

ISBN: 978-1-7342540-9-9

Copyright © 2021 by Muletta Hayes

All rights reserved. No part of this publication may be reproduced, distributed, or transmitted in any form or by any means, including photocopying, recording, or other electronic or mechanical methods without the prior written permission of the publisher. For permission requests, solicit the publisher via the address or website below.

R.D. Talley Books Publishing, LLC
4882 W. Lone Mountain Rd.
Las Vegas, Nevada 89130
www.rdtalleybooks.com

Dedication Page

First, I would like to give honor to God who is the head of my life. He has blessed me over and over again. I take nothing for granted. It is because of Him that I am.

To my grandchildren: Cameron, Aaliyah, James (Que), Amaryllis, Lazelle, and Se' Maj. May God continue to bless you and keep you. Grandma loves you unconditionally.

"You are my sunshine..my only sunshine. You make me happy when skies are grey. You'll never know dear...how much I love you… please don't take my sunshine away."

Hey, My Big Girl Aaliyah!!

To Barbara, Pamela and Anita…my sisters first, my cousins last, and always my friends. I love you guys!!

To my friend of over 35 years and counting, thanks Darius for all the love and support!

Contents

Inspirational Poetry

A Testimony 11

After The Tears 12

But God 14

Choir 15

Choose Ye This Day 16

Don't Turn Around 17

Empty Your Pockets 18

Enter To Worship, Depart To Serve 20

Evil Is All Around 22

From Head To Toe 23

God Is 24

God Is Your Protector 25

Good Night and Good Bye 26

Grace More Than We Deserve 28

He Is Coming With Clouds 30

Hold On 31

How Deep Is Your Praise? 32

I Rise 34

In His Presence 35

Is Your House Empty? 37

Jesus King of Kings 39

Keep The Faith 41

Lord, Hold On To Me 43

    Prayer 45

    Sometimes 47

    Spiritual Funnel 49

    The Holy Spirit Seal 51

    The Horsemen Are Coming 52

    There But For The Grace of God, Go I 53

    Time 56

    To My Child 57

    True 59

    What If? 61

    What Mark Will You Wear? 63

    What Really Happens When You're On Your Knees 66

    Working On My G.O.D 68

    Worship 70

    Your Day 40 Will Come 73

Mourning Losses

    Always Near 77

    Borrowed Heart 78

    Everywhere Is Me 79

    Forever In My Heart 81

    His Shield and Sword 82

    How Can I Let Go? 83

    I Am Still Near 85

    I'm Home 86

    It Will Be Too Late 87

    Little Angel 88

Missing You 89

Mother 91

My Little Box 92

Nathan 93

Plucked Too Soon 95

Time Heals All Pain 96

To Console Your Heart 98

Word To My Father 99

For The Holidays

28 Days 103

A Family On Thanksgiving 105

Because He Lives 106

Christmas Poem 107

Dr. Martin Luther King, Jr. 109

Father's Day 110

Free 112

Happy Valentine's Day To The Lonely Heart 113

It Isn't Fair 114

It's Not About Us 116

Let's Talk About Love 118

Motherless To Motherless 120

Mother's Day Poem To My Children 122

My Father, My Friend 123

Now We Are As One 125

Special Mother's Day Tribute 126

The Great I Am 128

The Man From Galilee 130

Dedication Pieces

A Blessed Birthday 135
A Blessing In Disguise 136
A Child Care Provider's Prayer 137
A Mother 139
A Mother, A Sister, A Friend 140
Admiration 141
God's Gift 142
Happy Birthday, Aunt Hilda 144
My Gifts 145
Poem For Barbara 146
Sisterly Love 148
Soul of A Typesetter 150
The Trial Of A Mother 151
To A Friend 152
To My Aunt With Love 153
To My Friend 154
To My Husband On Our Anniversary 155
To My Son On His Birthday 157
What If 159

Other Poems

A Bus Driver's Prayer 163
Am I My Brother's Keeper? 164
Born Again 166
Family 168

Freedom	169
Grandma's Words	170
I Am A Writer	171
I'm Not Tired	172
In His Name	173
Jesus, My All And All	175
Little Sheep Lost	176
Long Lost Love	177
Mrs. C	178
My Prayer	180
Night Shift	181
No Excuse	183
Please Be Kind	184
Portrait Of A Soul	186
Remember When	188
Senior	189
The Depression	190
The Ghost That Taunt Me	191
The Race	192
Too Late	193
What's In A Name?	195
When My Time Is Up	197
Final Dedication	198

Inspirational Poetry

A Testimony

I once was a lost soul
roaming among the many sheep
fumbling in the darkness
not knowing my hole was deep

But a voice whispered to me
"My child, turn to me;
a better life I can show you,
your spirit will be free."

At first, I hesitated
I was scared, I must admit
but I called on the name of Jesus
and a candle in my heart was lit

The light warmed my soul
it touched me deep within
He saved my world from falling
He allowed me to start again

So now, I let my light shine
so all people can see
how Jesus has been a blessing
and how he has saved me.

AFTER THE TEARS

So you stumbled across a heartache
a pain, a crushing despair
finding your back against a wall
thinking life isn't fair

You've stomped and you've yelled
cried until the water came out your ears
now you face the question
'What do you do after the tears?'

First, after you have cried
it's time to kneel and pray
to lose your mind for God
and let him have his way

Thank him for what he has done
what he's doing and going to do
remember, you belong to him
and he knows what's best for you

You are more than a conqueror
do not ever think less
an image of himself
too blessed to be stressed

In the Bible, it reads
'Anger and sin not'*
that means when you fight
you pray with all you've got

The battle is not yours
this is not a fleshly war
the Holy Spirit is your commander
he wants you even more

So, devil, you have no say
in my life, you are no longer
I have prayed to my God
my faith is getting stronger

No more, no more worries
tears will be shed
because Jesus saved me
when he hung, died and bled

I'm over it now
in the face of fears
I've learned how to fight
in spite of the tears.

Ephesians 4:26

But God!

Aches and pains seem to fill my day
I struggle sometimes but I press my way
I feel my life is hopped on a pod
oh my…But God!

The rent is due but the bank says no
the lights are off and the food is getting low
nothing but my faith and my rod
oh my…But God!

All alone, no one to see
wondering is it because of me
feeling lonely, depressed and odd
I was alone…But God!

God is my everything
I am because of him
I may hurt from time to time
but have use of all my limbs

He meets my need from day to day
He's my refuge by and by
comforting me, holding me
on those nights that I cry

Trials and tribulations may come
just look to the hills and nod
they're just to test you; don't fear
because there is always a…But God!

Choir

Make a joyful noise unto the Lord
sing his praise and lift him higher
acknowledge him even in song
and let your soul get caught on fire

Stand up in the choir stand
and let the congregation know
that wherever he may lead you
no questions asked, you will go

Open your heart and be glad
open your mouth with a song
you will see, his joy will spread
for the church will sing along

Work for the Lord
by using your hands and your voice
giving him praise
and in your heart rejoice

Let the words of the hymns
be another log on your fire
while you desire the will of God
as you sing on the church choir.

Choose Ye This Day

There's a driving force in everyone's life
a force that no man can see
whether it's God, the Holy Spirit
or the enemy with trickery

Everyone has a choice
to choose which one he feeds
the one that eats will grow
and in your life, it will lead

No man can serve two masters
for one you will love, the other hate
the choice is yours, free will
the choice to choose your fate

The Lord is coming like a thief in the night
we must be ready by what we say and do
he's coming when least expected
he prepared a place for me and you

In order to be ready, we must choose
whether to be ready or not
we must understand how frail we are
for some have seem to forgot

No one knows the day or hour
no time for your mind to be topsy turve
but the times have come to make a decision
choose ye this day in whom you will serve.

DON'T TURN AROUND

With my head up high
and my feet on the ground
I've come too far
to turn around.
There once was a time
in my life was confusion
my hopes were shattered
and my dreams were illusions.
But now I have changed
resumed into my books
trying to make a stand
avoiding the devil's hooks.
I'm just about there
my struggles about gone
realizing that there is better in me
I have to move on.
From a girl to a woman
no one said, easy it would be
but with self-determination
I'm going to see-
A brighter future for my children
and I'm going to let them know
that they too can make a difference
and it will show.
Just hold your head up high
and keep your feet on the ground
move on a little further
and don't turn around.

Empty Your Pockets

How can you even be mobile
with the heaviness you bear?
How can you breathe
when your stuff fumes the air?

Every time you go through
you stuff it in your pocket
way down under the lining
and once inside, you lock it

Heart aches and pains
stuffed way too deep
trials and tribulations
are not for you to keep

They're only there
to pass by or go through
not for you to hold on to
God will take them for you

He is our healer, redeemer
way maker and the light
whatever you need, he will supply it
and make everything all right

He has his hand out
for you to give him your all
all your worries, all your cares
He will catch you if you fall

It's time to empty your pockets
you are carrying too much stuff
time to say to yourself
'Enough is enough'

There's no need to carry all that stuff
and finding it hard to stand
just empty your pockets
inside the Master's Hand.

Enter To Worship, Depart To Serve

Enter His gates with thanksgiving
and His courts with praise
combined, that is called worship
acknowledging Him in all of your ways

Blocking out all of the distractions
filling your heart up to the rim
with thankfulness and gratefulness
concentrating totally on the goodness of Him

Your hands should be lifted up exalting, honoring
to Him, you need to bow down before
let your mouth be filled with praise
in utterance forever more

Your public worship should be a reflection
of your personal relationship at home
abiding in God's praise
and trusting you're never alone

Make a joyful noise unto the Lord
all ye in the lands
not sit and play the mannequin challenge
use your voice and your hands

Untainted worship is what we need
to serve unbelievers who are in the dark
ensuring them God's worthiness
and within their heart, leave His mark

God is spirit and his worshippers
must worship him in spirit and truth
Do you have his spirit?
How much of a worshipper are you?

So, as we enter His gates with thanksgiving
and His courts filled with praise as He deserves
remember true worship
for we enter to worship and depart to serve

Evil Is All Around

Every time I desire to do good
evil is all around
no matter what good I do
evil can be found.
I'm an outgoing person
I get along with everyone
I don't like to leave my work
until it is all done.
I'm what you call, A Pleaser
everyone has to be pleased
making people happy
makes me feel at ease.
That's impossible,
everyone can't be,
but people don't understand,
they want to get an attitude with me.
My job is my job
it's something I have to do,
whether it is happy
or sad for you.
To get along with everyone
I try to do my best
to treat you as a person
and put our problems to rest.
Just because
I may be no one to you
God created us all
and I'm someone too.

From Head To Toe

I will lift up mine eyes unto the hills
from where cometh my help
for he hears my cries, pities my moans
and answers whenever I yelp

My help comes from the Lord
who made heaven and made earth
who loves me unconditionally
who gave me my self-worth

He will not let your foot slip
He shall not slumber nor sleep
the Lord is your shade upon your right hand
us, in his hands he will keep

The sun shall not strike you by day
nor the moon by night
He shall protect you from all evil
and in you, be your light

He shall guard your going-out
and guard your coming-in
from this time until forever more
and that's the very end

Paraphrase, but that's The Word
for God, he said so
he's got you covered front and back
side to side, from head to toe.

God Is...

The light of God surrounds me
I know he is forever near
guiding my path daily
always giving an attentive ear

The love of God enfolds me
enclosing me with his comfort and care
cocooned in his bosom
trusting he is always there

The power of God protects me
keeping me safe, me…he preserves
securing me, blessing me, saving me
much more than I deserve

The presence of God watches over me
without a doubt, I know I'm his
His light, his love, power and presence
wherever I am, God is.

GOD IS YOUR PROTECTOR

Sometimes you may feel lost and confused
neglected, battered, beaten and bruised
but when in doubt, just trust in the Lord
for he will be your shield and sword

The coat of armor is what you can wear
when all is against you, he will be there
in time of need, pain and sorrow
he'll make it alright and fulfill your tomorrow

He will comfort, hold and keep you close
because he is the one who loves you the most
God knows all about you and what you can bear
no more will be put on you and nothing to fear

So, when the devil comes about
and in your mind, tries to fill it with doubt
tell him to flee and let God do the rest
you belong to him, he wants you to be blessed.

GOOD NIGHT AND GOOD BYE!

No matter how strong your faith
the devil will still try to discourage you
he will ride you like a bike
and blind you from your breakthrough

'Cause he loves the night
for in darkness, you cannot see
night doesn't always come at night
it represents where depression tends to be

Night makes it difficult
to see what's coming in the day
you're going to have to fight on your knees
and kneel to God and pray

For this is a spiritual warfare
it's not against flesh and blood
it's time to see the light God has for us
and not allow darkness to drag us through the mud

It's time to ask God
to come into our night
to cast out those familiar spirits
and to bring our daylight

The last thing the devil wants
is for you to get wise and take inventory
to talk to your father
and demand God's glory

So, if you're tired of your night
and you're seeking to revamp
just lean on our Savior
and let him light your lamp

For through him, we are saved
He is the true light, the El Shaddai
and with him we can say
to our darkness, good night and goodbye!

Grace...More Than We Deserve

Grace is God's way
to ravage, to rescue, to justly restore
grace changes us
our hearts, minds and attitudes better than before

For when grace happens
we receive from God a heart anew
He said in His Word, "I will give you a new heart
and put a new spirit within you."*

Instead of telling us to change, he creates it
He accepts us and cleans us up inside
He doesn't just want you to get into heaven
but in you, allow heaven to abide

God has sufficient grace
to meet every single challenge that tries to adhere
the tumbling, rumbling, reservoir of strength
and protection
his grace dethrones your fear

As a result of this powerful grace
we can trust God's love for us is never-ending
to him you're worth loving, worth having
allow him to do the healing and mending

Know that at this very instant
you are loved, not because you please him or try and fail
but he desires to be your father
and in your life, to prevail

For by grace, we have been saved through faith
a gift from God, nothing we've done
He gives us grace, he gives us mercy
and he gave us his only begotten son

Loved, accepted, adopted
and also we, his children, he conserves
giving us grace greater than we can imagine
and much more than we deserve.

Ezekiel 36:26

HE IS COMING WITH CLOUDS

Dear child of mine
whom I love so much
don't use the man-made things
as your crutch.
Use your heart
open it up and let me in
so that you too
may be born again.
I hung on the cross
and died for your sins
hoping your heart will love
and you'd be disciplined.
Give me some time
maybe an hour or two
a life you'd see
that you never knew.
I hear your soul crying
a longing so strong
in my palace
is where you belong.
So, get your soul ready
I'm coming as I vowed
like a thief in the night
I'm coming with clouds.

"Look, he is coming with the clouds," and "every eye will see him, even those who pierced him"; and all peoples on earth "will mourn because of him." So shall it be! Amen.
-Revelations 1:7

Hold On

When it seems you've lost your way
and from Him, you went astray
when all hope seems bleak or gone
just cling to him and just hold on

When it seems the roads are rough
and you feel you have had enough
when life is a struggle, your faith, your mourn
just grab his hand and just hold on

When the devil seems to put you through
remember that God sent his son for you
just trust and believe there is a new dawn
keep the faith and just hold on

He knew you before you were you
and all that you would go through
all the aches, pains, and rips torn
and that you would need to just hold on

So, when you feel that no one cares,
or that He is not there,
when you kneel down to pray
and don't know the words to say,
when you feel all hope is lost
and every night you turn and toss,
just trust and know that your redeemer lives
and with you, he wants a bond
He brought you to it, he will bring you through it
faint not, and just HOLD ON!

How Deep Is Your Praise?

To praise is to express
to convey, to be deep and true
to squeeze out, press out
what is deep inside of you.
Praise is the offering
of grateful homage in words and song
special honor shown privately and publicly
when it's heartfelt, it's never wrong.

You can praise with your voice
your hands, your feet, a cymbal
just know when you praise God
the demons fear and tremble.
When praises go up, blessings come down
changes will take place
praise him in the midst of your trials
praise him for his mercy and grace.

Praise him in the hallway
if you can't get through the door
and if you find yourself feeling faint
praise him even more.

We were created and destined
for all of our earthly days
to lift our hands and worship
and fill our mouths with praise.

So, let us confluence in this church
as our hearts are reassured
let everything that has breath
praise ye the Lord.
There's no room for idle time
there should be no delays
because God is an awesome God
How deep is your praise?

I Rise

With every stone tossed at me,

    I Rise.

With every tongue lashed at me,

    I Rise.

With every back turned on me,

    I Rise.

I Rise, I Rise, I Rise

With the grace of God,

    I Rise.

In His Presence

Have you ever been in his presence
and you didn't want to leave?
All he wanted to give
you wanted to receive

Your tears began to fall
and soon they begin to flow
because the spirit starts to speak
and you know that you know, that you know

It was nobody but God
that brought you along the way
that kept you, that saved you
that brought you on today

In his presence there's peace
tranquility and love
the bare essence of his grace
from the master up above

Once in his presence
is not enough for one
you'll want to be there every minute
you can get with the son

In his presence to worship
and be a vessel for his glory
letting his light shine in you
and your life tell his story

Oh, to be used by God
and let the world see his glow
living for his purpose with you
in your life, it will show

So, it's time to get ugly for God
as most folks would say
get in God's presence
and let him have his way.

Is Your House Empty?

When you clean your house of unclean spirits
the spirits walk around looking for rest
noticing you did not fulfill its place
it then comes back and possess

It not only welcomes itself back in
but it does not come alone
it brings friends with it, seven at least
to you, it's quite unknown

But once you clean your house within
and fill it with fruit and bread
the fruits of the spirits, the bread of life
these spirits will not be fed

The spirit of love, joy, goodness
faithfulness, gentleness and peace
kindness, self-control and forbearance
will make the spirits cease

For what good is a beautiful mansion,
what is its worth when love doesn't reside?
A king-sized bed, wall to wall carpet
it's just empty if God doesn't abide

When you have been delivered
and your house is now clean
you should hunger and thirst for God to fill it
and on him, you now lean

So, get your house in order
clean it, let God come in and sup
Is your house empty?
If so, let God reside and fill it up.

JESUS, THE KING OF KINGS

At times we may not see
why tribulations come our way
but knowing in our hearts
from Jesus, we did go astray

But isn't it a blessing
to know he's forever there?
No matter the circumstance
he handles what you can't bear

To give away your burdens
and let God handle it all
to open his arms wide
to catch you when you fall

To hear his sweet voice saying,
"Child of mine, come to me,
give me your heart and I
will give you love eternally."

A God so generous
giving us his only son
never leaving you alone
or his work undone

There is no price to pay
there is nothing we lost
for Jesus paid it all
when he died on the cross

You can open your heart
and let Jesus in
let him take over
so you can start life again.

Keep The Faith

I can't begin to imagine
how it must be for you
your cup is filled to the rim
with all the things that you do

People tend to get the green eye
when they see someone on top
they push your buttons
and it seems they never stop

Being the soft-hearted person you are
your feelings are sensitive, you cry
you fall on bending knees
and ask the Lord, "Why?"

I wouldn't be a friend if I kept quiet
and I mean every word I say
they're going to talk more tomorrow
than what they do today

They'll pick and they'll joke
until they think that you are weak
for you to be down
is what they seek

But you stay strong
as the old hymn says, Stand Still
for God knows it all
what comes, let it be at his will

I know I am just
an outsider looking in
dry your eyes, keep the faith
I am also your friend.

Lord, Hold On To Me

If my mouth seems as if
it wants to fly away,
or I don't know
the right words to say,
when I get angry
and want to yell or shout,
when I don't obtain control
of what comes out…

Lord, hold on to me.

When my hands seem to get idle
and I don't know what to do,
knowing in my heart
they should be praying to you…

Lord, hold on to me.

When my heart gets cold
and my neighbor, I don't think of,
when my heart is raged with anger
that should be replaced with love…

Lord, hold on to me.

When my way seems unclear
and I get confused and lose my way,
when the road that I choose
seems to lead me astray,
when my soul cries out

and my heart aches with pain,
when I feel all my living
was a life lived in vain,
when I think there is no one
who knows the burdens that I bear,
when I think there isn't a soul
who can truly understand and care…

Lord, hold on to me.

PRAYER

Prayer is essential
in your walk with Christ
our Christian life should begin with prayer
to call to God, for he sacrificed

Prayer is a simple conversation
that you have with God one on one
developing a close relationship
just a talk with the Father and the Son

In our prayer, we need to praise
let God know that we know he is great
He is the Alpha and Omega
the author and finisher of our faith

We need to present ourselves
as we're praying, we're seeking God's Will
reading his Word, learning more of his way
learning to be still

We need provision in our prayer
knowing he will provide every need
trusting him to care
and for others, we intercede

We need to profess our sins
asking for forgiveness,
keeping the relationship pure and good
forgiving others just as well
as we know Jesus would

Last, but not least
we need to ask for protection when we pray
we need his guidance, his loving hand
for our walk each and every day

Even if you're lost and confused
or if you don't know what words to say
let your heart speak to God
and kneel to him and pray

For he knows your heart
and all that you can bear
just trust in your Father
and come to him in prayer.

SOMETIMES

There is so much going on
so much on your mind
your life is topsy turvy
and peace is hard to find

You struggle day to day
your soul hunger and thirst
little did you know
you failed to put God first

Although you sometimes pray
and you sometimes read his Word
you sometimes praise his name
but sometimes is unheard

You sometimes went to church
you sometimes gave of yourself
you sometimes witnessed
but mostly put him on a shelf

He's not a 'sometimes' God
He is a God that's Holy and true
He does not want you sometimes
He wants all of you

There is no such thing as too busy
that God is not the most part
if this is a description of you
then you need to re-evaluate your heart

As long as you have breath
please do not hesitate
don't put in your mind, 'yeah, tomorrow…"
for tomorrow may be too late

Your day can start today
He can create in you a new
He gave you all you need to worship
so now it's up to you

Every tongue is going to confess
and every knee is going to bow
don't let another day pass you by
let your 'all the time' begin right now.

Spiritual Funnel

There are two types of rain: natural and spiritual
one is where water falls, and on the ground, it rests
the other is where righteousness and abundance fall
and you are blessed

In the natural, you use an umbrella
to block the rain from afloat
in the spiritual, you need a funnel to catch it all
but some still carry a little tote

Righteousness and blessings
permeates abundance and refresh who is abound
like how rain is to a dry, parched
and very thirsty ground

Storm clouds may come your way
but they don't always mean dark days ahead
to your life, there may even be a time
the water you will have to tread

The flashing clouds often thought of as frightening
and what they represent
also comes into our lives
just before blessings and refreshment

If there are dark clouds right now
don't despair, just maintain
thank the Lord for the clouds
and get on your knees and pray for rain

But in this rain that will fall
don't use an umbrella or duck into a tunnel
but believe it and receive it
with your spiritual funnel.

THE HOLY SPIRIT SEAL

Do you have the authentic seal within your heart
that shows your relationship with God is real?
The final stamp embedded inside…
The Holy Spirit Seal

Our sign of authenticity showing we belong to God
is his Holy Spirit which abides within
his spirit helps us when we pray
and brings forth God's character
in our lives that we walk in

His spirit empowers us to overcome sin
and gives us strength to do things we couldn't dream
his spirit comforts us in our brokenness
and makes God's presence in our lives beam

His spirit is the truest sign that we are his
and we trust and we do believe
his spirit blesses us each and every day
his spirit, we need to receive

So, if your authenticity seal is missing
or you don't know where to begin
it's time to get your house in order
it's time to allow God to abide within.

The Horsemen Are Coming

So, you think you're running hard
you whimper and complain
but if you're weeping in the sunshine,
what are you going to do when it rains?

What are you going to do
when your horsemen come?
Put on the whole armor of God and fight,
or will you just go numb?

It's time to get prayed-up
let the holy spirit abide within
take a sip of your cup
it's the only way to win

Right now, it's subtle
the foremen are meek
the real fight is coming
and it wants to find you weak

But if you're falling apart
because of small things today,
what about the big ones
the ones that are on their way?

Time to wipe your tears and be strong
no time for hum-drumming
get prayed-up, holy ghost filled
because the horsemen are coming.

THERE BUT FOR THE GRACE OF GOD, GO I

You find reasons to complain
about all that's not right
negatively speaking and wasted energy
as you struggle and fight

Selfishly focusing on your wants
not thankful for what you've got
or things that could have went wrong
but yet, they did not

God knows what you can bear
He created you with love
but it's time for you to sit and think
about all the could'ves…

It could have been you
diagnosed with something with no cure
your health dangling by a thread
and your future is unsecure

You could've been the one
whose life changed in a blink
an uncontrollable accident
and your family's heart sink

You could've been the person
whose life is in the street
strung-out on drugs
with no home and no food to eat

You could've been molested
or may have, by Uncle Sam or Uncle Don
but you're here to tell your story
and testify that life does go on

You could've been the person
whose picture flash upon the screen
who has not been heard of
and has a last date they were seen

Strung-out, homeless
desolate, molested, dead and gone
alcoholic, car accident
but God allowed you to live on

Don't worry about who walked out
thank God for those who stayed
don't concern yourself with naysayers
but thank him for those who prayed

God is our anchor, our support
although we may hurt, he heals
he's our stronghold, our protector
and his children, he conceals

He didn't unleash everything
that the devil wanted to do
the devil wanted to kill and destroy you
but God blocked it for you

So, as you are thanking him
and praising him for all that you've got
thank him for blocking all the things
that could've went wrong, but did not

Thank you, Lord, for your divine protection
to allow me to be, not die
for covering me under your precious blood
there but for the grace of God, go I.

TIME

It's time to stop playing church
time is winding down, get off the wall
it's time to be about our father's business
it's you and I that he has called

To do his will on earth
disciples and fishers of men
spreading his gospel of truth
until he comes back again

Every morning when he awakes you
you're blessed with a day of change
to choose life or death
it's time to rearrange

It's time to set things in order
get your soul straight
there's not one minute to spare
there's no room to procrastinate

There's a journey we must face
and time is at hand
pray without ceasing, your blessing increasing
and when confused, just stand

Don't wait for the trumpet to sound
to figure out your reason or rhyme
get busy for the Lord now
while there's still breath and you have time.

TO MY CHILD

When you look into a mirror,
what exactly do you see?
Do you see all the beauty,
the strength and integrity?

Do you see all the struggles
that in your life came along?
That made you who you are,
more confident and strong?

Do you see all the tribulations
that tested you left and right,
which made you re-evaluate
and come to me through the night?

Do you see love, peace, joy
and mere beauty to behold?
a life worth dying for
that's worth more than gold?

At times, things may get hard
there are a lot of challenges to face
but with strength and determination
you too can win this race

Even when you're hurting
or feel no one is there
my heart is open, my ears are listening
and I am one who cares

You are never alone
don't even think this so
I love you more than words can say
more than you'll ever know

If one day you feel as though
your back is against the wall
just come to me and you will see
I will take care of it all

You are my child and please believe
the love I have is true
that is why I opened my arms
and whole-heartedly died for you

And if those things are not mirrored
and them you fail to see
re-check your mirror, my child
because they are apparent to me

An image of myself
I created you to be
when all is lost, pick up your cross
and begin to follow me.

                         Love, Jesus

TRUE

A true Christian follows Jesus' commandments
and not just in him, believe
they know church community is standard to their faith
not just attend on holidays and then leave

They read their Bible regularly
not just when times get tough
they give thanks, no matter the circumstance
not just pray when things get rough

They work to make their lifestyle
resemble the Bible through the Holy Spirit
not twist the Lord's words
so that to their lifestyle, it will fit

They will sacrifice regardless
whatever may come their way
not just sacrifice when it's convenient
no matter the risk, their tithes, they will pay

A true Christian holds fast against temptation
under pressure, their faith stays strong
they'll show their faith despite the scenario
and in their heart, sing a song

A true Christian not just knows of Jesus
but desires in them, for him to stir
they know him for themselves
as their Lord and Savior

There are religious people and there are Christians
the religious just go with the flow
but a true Christian worships
because they know that they know, that they know

It's time for self-examination
to examine the Christian in you
Are you who they say you are?
Are you religious, or are you true?

WHAT IF...

What if you awoke this morning
to find that you were left behind,
your entrance to the kingdom of God
was annulled and declined?

The rapture had came and went
and here you are, face to face
without any mercy
and without any grace

Would you fall to your knees
and beg to be saved,
wanting a second chance
and have your sins waived?

Would you cry out to the Lord
praising his holy name,
tears rolling down your face
your head bowed in shame?

Worshipping him in his glory
thanking him all the day
wanting him to use you
kneeling to him and pray

The time is at hand
you have your second chance
you awoke this morning, point blank
so praise him in advance

Praise and worship him
with a heart filled with cheer
for the time is soon to come
when the rapture is here

Be ye also ready
don't let your work be caught undone
for your heart should long
to be with the Father and the Son

What if you awoke this morning
to find you were left behind?
Would you change how you lived?
Would your life be redefined?

So, why wait until the last minute,
pushing God away?
While the blood is running warm in your veins
tomorrow is not promised…do it today.

WHAT MARK WILL YOU WEAR?

As the end draws near
and the first rapture starts
while the saints are drawn-up
and we are divided apart

What mark will you wear
when it's finally here?
Your decision has to be quick
the time is near

Will you still be on earth
crying out for the Lord,
seeking protection
from his shield and sword?

Trying to be saved
but having to first die
yearning for salvation
and all night, you cry

Living with the beast
and at Satan's scorn
wishing in your heart
that you were reborn

Will you wear the mark
of the beast within,
and be at his command
still living in sin?

Making hell your home
and being cast into the lake of fire,
be at his will
a demon for hire?

Or will you wear
the most precious seal?
One so powerful
in your soul, you can feel

By not studying God's Word
and doing his work on earth
keeping your faith in our Lord
and all of its worth

Making heaven your home
and in your soul rejoice
How can you even consider
deciding on a choice?

There's not much time
the rapture is on it's way
give yourself to Jesus
and do it today

Because not before long
you will have to decide
there is no where to run
and no place to hide

The rapture is coming
guaranteed, you'll be there
but the question is
What mark will you wear?

What Really Happens When You're On Your Knees

As soon as you submit
and have it in your mind to pray
the devil gets busy
and sends his demons your way

Trying to deter you
and cloud your mind
because he seeks to devour
all that he finds

But as you slowly bend
and your knees hit the floor
fold your hands, bow your head
the devil can't mess with you anymore

For as your words come out of your mouth
and you talk to the Son
He guards over your soul
a war has begun

As you say 'Amen'
and your prayer is done
one battle down
and for you, it is won

Prayer is the key
to keeping the devil at bay
so before life hits you hard
kneel down and pray

Pray in the morning, at noon and at night
your prayer will get you through
always talking to God
so much, that the devil fears you.

WORKING ON MY G.O.D.

Studying God's Word
and what he has laid out for me
can't hold me back
I'm working on my G.O.D.

Constantly in prayer
worshipping is the key
no slowing down now
I'm working on my G.O.D.

Being his servant
spreading the gospel happily
joyful and content
I'm working on my G.O.D.

Letting the world know
all he has done for me
keeping my faith
I'm working on my G.O.D.

Setting my sight on paradise
no, not earthly
humbly…
I'm working on my G.O.D.

Chains falling off
finally set free
sighs of relief
I'm working on my G.O.D.

Praising his name
no place I'd rather be
than pleasing my Lord
and working on my G.O.D.

Worship

You sit there in church
with a smug look upon your face
believing your alarm clock woke you
and you got yourself to this place

How can you even think
that it's all about you?
it's because of His grace and mercy
that you can start anew

Your worshipping is in vain
if your heart don't say yes
he doesn't care about your little
he only wants your best

So, don't wave your hand
as if you don't have use of your limb
you were blessed to confess
so if you can, stand and acknowledge him

God is a jealous God
the commandments tells us so
99.5% won't do, he wants ALL of you
from your head down to your toe

Times are getting hard
there's no room for despair
it's time to look to the Father
and turn to him in prayer

This world is not your home
it's just a stop on your way to glory
you were born to worship him
and to continue his story

It's time to stop living for self
being mean, hateful and lies
these are all Satan's tools
and you, he despise

So, stop playing church
allowing the devil to play you
using you, abusing you
and putting your life through

Trust and believe
God's on your side, he loves you more
you're on his mind day and night
and it is you he adores

I understand your skepticism
Could this really be true?
Yes, it is, he loves you so
that he sent his only son to die for you!

You may think your worth is not much
but, oh my God, to him
you're precious within his sight
a diamond, a precious gem

So, raise your hand in honor
and sing praises to his name
ask him to come into your heart
and you won't be the same

You'll stop playing church
your life with him will begin anew
living for our savior
finding a new creature within you

Getting through struggles is hard
but worship is the key
I don't know about you
but I don't want rocks crying out for me.

Your Day 40 Will Come

One of the hardest things to do
is to patiently wait
the carnal side of us
wishes to decide our own fate

But greater is coming
when we wait upon the Lord with good cheer
be patient, let God,
your day 40 is near

You've been praying for that promotion
you know the job belongs to you
but it doesn't seem like it's happening
so the head man, you chew

Not knowing it was coming
the one for you that was assigned
you lost hope, couldn't cope
on your day 39

Lord, send me a spouse
of your image, I do pray
but your patience grew very thin
and your faith began to stray

Little did you know
for only a while you would wait
but instead you settled
on your day 38

You prayed for a car
you asked for favor too
you believed in your heart
that God will see you through

But then somehow
you fell for the devil's tricks
you waited no more,
missed your blessing on day 36

We seem to forget
that it's all God's plan
He is the master
our blessings are in his hands

How are you supposed to know
that your blessings are on their way?
It's called faith, my friend
and from it, don't go astray

Patience is of the essence
He has way more than a crumb
just wait on the Lord
your day 40 will soon come.

Mourning Losses

Always Near

I saw you, mother dear
as you laid in your bed and wept
I saw you as you passed my room
I saw you as you slept

I know how hard these last days have been
I can't imagine how you must feel
it's almost as if you are dreaming
and the reality is not real

You probably imagine me
still at school in my dorm
you might even pretend
that I'm tucked in my bed and warm

I am in a better place
there is no other one I'd like to be
my dorm is now the kingdom of heaven
my soul has been set free

The bond that we shared
will never start to decay
the tears that you weep for me
I will spiritually wipe them away

Please take comfort in knowing
a weak, a month, a year
I will not leave you
for I will always be near.

Borrowed Heart

Time passes by so quickly
and things happen we don't understand,
but it's a comfort to know
that it is all in God's hand.
You don't belong to anyone
you, yourself, don't even belong to you,
you're just a soul borrowed from God
and a testimony with what you go through.
To borrow means to give back
and in our hearts we must remember,
embedded on our soul is a tag
and it reads, 'Return to Sender'.
We were blessed to have had
the time that God allowed us to be,
his struggle is now over
and his soul is set free.
His memory will forever live in our lives,
he did impact,
he was a heart borrowed
we had to give him back.

Everywhere Is Me

Even though I'm no longer with you
there's no place I'd rather be,
If you look around, I never left...
for everywhere is me...

If you look up in the sky
and see a star shining so bright
it is me guiding you
in the hour of midnight

The sun you see which gleams
bright yellow like gold
is me keeping you warm
on the days that you are cold

The tingle that you feel
deep within your heart
is my love for you
for the time that we're apart

When you hear rustling of the leaves
and the wind begins to blow
that is my way of speaking
to spiritually say hello

If your days aren't always sunny
and rain seems to appear
just close your eyes and think of me
for I will always be near.

When the sun goes down
and all is gone with day light
I will be the blanket that comforts you
and gently kiss you goodnight

Please don't cry, I know it's hard
for your heart is completely tore
I love you all as you love me
but God loved me more.

Forever In My Heart

Words cannot express
the pain that's in my heart
a constant piercing pain
when, from a loved one, we depart

We didn't want to see you in pain
we didn't want you to shed a tear
so God stepped in
and we didn't interfere

He saw you in pain
He heard your every moan and groan
He didn't want to see you suffer
so he took you on home

This is not really goodbye
it's just a short time we're apart
until we see each other again
you will forever be in my heart.

His Shield and Sword

I'm sorry I did not say goodbye
I apologize for the pain
but I had to leave all of you
because Jesus called my name

He wanted me to follow him
and to sit at his side
I had a seat in his kingdom
and my needs would be supplied

He told me not to worry
for my family would understand
in time, they will be comforted
to know I'm in his hand

My leaving was unexpected
but my living was not in vain
my work on earth was done
I could no longer remain

I love you all very much
but I had to get my reward
heaven is now my home
I'm protected by his shield and sword.

How Can I Let Go?

A precious gift from above
A gift I do not yet know,
How can I hold on so tight?
Yet, how can I let go?
You have to understand
I'm alone and not quite free
this unplanned event
was never meant to be
I know it's hard to imagine
that the love I feel is so great
you are a part of me,
the me that I did create
An angel in disguise
a love so tremendous and true
you are probably asking yourself,
'Why it had to be you?'
Please don't feel at fault
please don't feel to blame
I couldn't give you a life
nevertheless, a given name
Maybe if my situation
was different in a way,
maybe we'll be together
in another life someday
My mind and heart are fighting
over this decision I must face
How can I be cruel
with the life I must erase?

I'm not authorized
to kill or not kill
but because of my tribulations
it has got to be done at will
So, my little angel
who is more precious than gold,
the baby I don't know
but am dying to hold,
I cannot bear to think
of the thought of losing you
but please remember
my love for you is true
Although it's going to be hard
but my conscience at least will know
in Jesus' bosom you will be
and I have to let go.

I Am Still Near

I saw your mother dear
stop in the middle of your step,
thoughts of me entered your mind
I saw you while you wept.
I watched you as you lay in bed
at the ceiling you did stare,
tossing and turning, hoping and praying
I saw, because I was there.
Sleepless nights, foggy days
fills up your life today,
I'm sending you some comforting words
to let you know that I'm okay.
I love you very much
but this you already know,
it pains me just the same
of trying to let you go.
Some days you may feel a touch
or a wind may blow a tree,
close your eyes and reminisce
for it is only me.
Death will never change our love
even though we're apart,
I never really left you
because we'll always be in each other's hearts.
So, on this Mother's Day
please don't shed a tear
remember all the love we have
and know that I am near.

I'm Home

God was looking around his kingdom
and he saw an empty space
He went in search of an angel
to fill in its place

He looked around and saw you
with a heart made of gold
more lovely than sunset
and beauty to behold

He saw that you were aching
with pain you didn't need
you've done your work on earth my good servant
you've done your deed

To prove your work was not in vain
although from your family, you'd be apart
He wanted you in his kingdom
so he touched your loving heart

God makes no mistakes
and we know this to be true
we wanted you to be with us
but he saw an angel in you

He brought you in our lives
but didn't promise you would stay
even though you're no longer with us
we'll see you again someday.

It Will Be Too Late

Do not weep for me
when my body is cold
and I can no longer speak.
Do not bring me flowers
to my homegoing service
when you never took the time
to bring them to me while I was alive.
Do not lean over my casket
wishing I could get up,
for when I was among the living,
not once did you show that you cared.
Do not gaze upon my closed eyes
and my frozen face
wishing I could speak,
for when I did,
you did not listen.
Do not hope for a sign of relief
for your conscience,
by the time you decide to care
it will then be too late.

LITTLE ANGEL

Conceived into a womb
you were special from the start
implanted there for me
with a piece of Jesus' heart.
My heart was filled with joy
from the bottom of my soul
more precious than life
with the upmost beauty to behold.
Life has took a turn
for God wanted you more,
he must have seen your smile
and your cute cheek that I adored.
He took you into his bosom
and gave you love eternally
the love I would have gave
if only you belonged to me.
My sweet little angel
with a message, 'Return to Sender'
God's gift returned
and I could not surrender.
I know you'll always be with me
little sweet angel of mine,
until I see you again,
"Peace be Thine".

Missing You

As time went by, I watched you grow
into the young man you came to be
you were special right from the start
you possessed a little bit of me

You made me so proud over the years
as you matured and went on your own
it seemed as if you were still a child
but in reality, you were grown

You're my son's child; my grandson
but still mine, just the same
my heart has been overflowing
since, into my life, you came

But life has taken a turn
for God loved you more
He wanted you with him in his kingdom
and on you, his love he would pour

He knew that we would be hurting
and we would miss your loving touch
He promised to send us a comforter
for he loved you just as much

It was much too soon for you to go
but God, he knows what's best
for the time that we did have
we were richly blessed

We will miss you dearly
during the time that we're apart
but the comforting memories that I have
will forever be in my heart.

MOTHER

God makes no mistakes
this I know
even though the pain is piercing
I have to let go.
But in my heart
you will always be,
for you were more
than just a mother to me.
Memories of you
will never fade away,
I will forever cherish them
each and every day.
A virtuous woman indeed
my mother, my friend
rubies can't compare
to your heart within.
Sadly missed you will be
our hearts are tore
our love for you is great,
but God loved you more.

MY LITTLE BOX

In my little pink box
all in neatly fold
are all of my obituaries
and the stories they told

Each of my loved ones
and ones who touched my life
I sit on my bed and read them
although they cut like a knife

When I miss someone
who has gone and passed away
I sit and read their obituary
and hope to see them again someday.

NATHAN

Nathan is a little boy
who, in June, would have been four
but holidays and birthdays
he won't see anymore

You see, his mother had a problem
she used drugs abruptly
she never thought for a second
that it would affect her baby

She always came home high
without even a care
Nathan stayed hungry
because their cupboard was bare

His father was no better
he drank his paycheck away
until his roaring temper
exploded that day

The alcohol had taken over him
and his attitude turned to anger
little Nathan had no idea
that his life was in danger

He was buried in a little brown casket
all dressed in blue
with words of remanences
and a lot of 'we're going to miss you'

His father went to jail
his mother still high on drugs
if only instead of getting high
she gave her baby love

Oh, little Nathan…
I know it's hard to see
but very much so
in reality, you are free.

PLUCKED TOO SOON

God was looking around his garden
and he saw an empty space
He went in search of a flower
to fill into its place

He saw you here on earth
so meek, humble and bold
He decided you would be perfect
although your life had just unfold

He noticed his image in you
and the amazing qualities that you show
He loved the way you'd light up a room
so he knew his garden would grow

God makes no mistakes
this we know to be true
we saw the earthly man
but he saw a perfect flower in you

A very special flower
whose life was so in tune
just beginning to unfold itself
a flower plucked too soon.

Time Heals All Pain?

Does time heal all pain?
That's what everyone say
I was once a believer
until that cold December day

My aunt stepped into the room
sadness was all over her face
tears filled her eyes
as her heart began to race

"Do you know the meaning of death?"
she asked in a pale, tearful way
with fear in my heart racing madly
on that cold December day

I pretended to tie my boots
as she told me about my mother
she began to cry and hold me tight
as I wondered about my sister and brother

I didn't look into her face
because I was scared I'd cry too
so, I just bent over once again
and pretended to tie my shoe

I went to school that morning
with a feeling of being alone
I sat at my desk and cried
so, the principal sent me home

'My mother is gone', I thought
she won't be with me again
although I was only seven
my world felt like the end

She won't be able to wipe my tears
or bandage my knee when I fall
she won't be able to kiss me goodnight
or answer when I call

My body suddenly became numb
my mind blank, nothing to say
I remember as if it were this morning
that cold December day

Twenty-two years have come and gone
but yet the pain still remains
there are things that time cannot heal
and the pain stays the same

Time does not heal all pain
but that's what people say
I once was a believer
until that cold December day.

To Console Your Heart

I know that you are hurting
I can't imagine the pain you bare,
God promised to send a comforter
and to always be there.

Losing a loved one is hard
only time can heal and mend,
but please keep in mind
that this is not the end.

No one was promised to us
they were lent for just a little while,
to be there for companionship
and brighten our day with their smile.

But as humans we grow attached
and when God calls them home,
we hurt, cry, feel distraught
and feel that we are all alone.

Isn't it good to know
that again these loved ones we will see,
and the pain and hurt we once felt
will finally be set free.

But until that time comes to us
to console your aching heart
although we love him, God loved him more
it's just a little while that you are apart.

Words To My Father

I saw you father dear
as you paced across the floor
although you had a few answers
you wanted to know more
I saw the quiet tears
you would often try to hide
I even felt when I left
a part of you that died
I hope my words of comfort
be embedded in your heart
to soothe and cradle you
for the time that we're apart
You always wanted the best for me
ever since the age of four
unbelievably, I have the best
God even gave me more
I have a seat in his kingdom
sitting on a throne
He is always by my side
and I am never alone
I know how difficult and how hard
my leaving so soon must be
you always thought in your mind
you would leave before me
That's what parents think
they would go before their son
but it's not the age that matters
it's when your work on earth is done

I saw you, father dear
as you paced across the floor
I know how much you love me
but God loved me more.

For The Holidays

28 Days

February is the month set aside for us to honor and
celebrate the lives of our people
like Rosa Parks, Harriet Tubman, and Dr. King,
to teach the children the history of our ancestors
and what their lives to us mean

Just 28 days out of 365
to recognize the lives of our Legacy
how they fought, paved the way
and tried to make things better for you and me

How Harriet freed the slaves, Jackie broke barriers
and how Malcolm fought for our rights,
how Mae went into space
and how Garrett Morgan invented the traffic light

The Harlem Renaissance and the burning of churches
where the enemy played a part,
Madam CJ helped our hair care
and Daniel Williams performed the first open heart

Just 28 days, we have inventors and heroes and musicians
Louis Armstrong, Ella Fitzgerald, Billie Holiday
and let's not forget Nina or Ray,
who went ahead and started the journey
for our entertainers we have today.

Just 28 days to talk about Langston Hughes
Gwendolyn Brooks and Maya Angelo too
just a few poets who told their story
and all that they went through

I stand here on the 28th day to let you know
our history remains to be unfold
The wounds, the transgressions,
our fight and our struggle needs to be told

We can't do it in just 28 days
and we shouldn't limit our history
to just that time we borrow,
because our history is way too important to put-off
especially to our children, for our history is their
tomorrow.

A Family On Thanksgiving

Thanksgiving is a time
for families to come near
the season for love to surface
that once was covered throughout the year

A time for joy and comfort
a time to know you're blessed
to bury the quarrels and disagreements
and let love manifest

But it's very hard to do
when you live so far away
although your heart is with them
it's not the same this holiday

You can't hear their laughter
and the joy, you're not able to feel
you're sad and blue, your heart aches
this depressed feeling you must conceal

But a spirit of relief comes within
to allow you to celebrate once more
to remind you of all the love
and what to truly be thankful for

So, on this holiday, I send
my heart in the place of my absentee
whether absent, present, near or far
we're forever a family.

Because He Lives

Today is not about a bunny or eggs
but it's about three nails and a cross
it's not about a basket or a hunt
but about saving souls that were loss

It's about a Redeemer
who sacrificed his life for you
it's about a Savior
who wanted to create in you a new

It's about a love so pure,
so unconditional…so deep
that he gave up his life
so our life, we may keep

It's about the blood that was shed
that carried our names with each drop
it's about a connection, a power
that will never stop

It's about the empty tomb
and the cloth on the floor
it's about the goodness
that he came to restore

We celebrate today
because 3 days ago, the sacrifice Jesus did give
and now we rejoice
because He lives!!

Christmas Poem

"You better watch out, you better not pout,
You better not cry, I'm telling you why",
is what parents recite every year
to instill in their children
and try to put fear

But I think it's sad
and I think it's odd
that they would rather them fear Santa
than to fear God

Wanting their names on the good list,
they strife…
not one concern
for the good book of life

Being happy that Santa
leaves presents in disguise
but not teaching them that
God blesses them when he opens their eyes

On Christmas Eve night
they wait with anticipation and glee
no thought in their mind
it's all about a savior who set us free

Not just children I speak of
it's adults too who miss
they take this special day
and commercialize this

Forgive them, Father
for they apparently know not
to be blessed with what they have
and all that they've got

It's nice to exchange presents
to show each other love
but let's not forget
it's about our Savior up above

Who was born on this day
for a purpose and a reason
He is the reason
we celebrate this season!

DR. MARTIN LUTHER KING

Today we come together
to honor and remember a strong black man
who wanted and fought for equality
for us to walk hand in hand

As he marched for our freedom
dogs were released, water was sprayed
incarcerated for the color of his skin
but not once was he afraid

He spoke on nonviolence
replacing it with love and peace
he stood for equal rights
he wanted the discrimination to cease

He believed all men were created equal
not one left behind
this strong black man
was also loving, gentle and kind

Wanting to do God's Will
a soldier for the Lord nonstop
always trusting, always believing
we're going to reach that mountaintop

Let's remember his words today
overcoming and let freedom ring
a great man who took a stand and fought for our rights
rest in peace, Dr. Martin Luther King.

Father's Day

Our Father, who art in heaven
hallowed be thy name
The Father, The Son, The Holy Ghost
The Holy Trinity…all in one, all the same

A loving father who knows you deeply
even the number of hairs on your head
who knew you before you were in your mother's womb
your purpose, your life…all spirit led

He promised to never leave you
to always be by your side
and where you need to be
trust in him and he will guide

He wants to bless you abundantly
and as on His Word you hungrily feast,
He will fill you up with joy
and give your mind and soul peace

Our Father, the One True God
with all power in his hand
who gives us all that we need
and helps us when we need to stand

You can lean on him in times of trouble
you can run to him and hide
He wants you to be a part of him
and in you, he will abide

He loves you on your worst day
to him you are a gem
it doesn't matter who you are, where you are
you are his child and you belong to him

So, on this Father's Day
I rejoice with comfort and love
shouting, praising and worshipping
honoring my Heavenly Father up above.

FREE

On July 4, 1776
Congress declared the USA free,
the declaration of independence for all
except whose skin color looked like me

Some of us still celebrate
naive to the history of us
forgetting that our ancestors were still slaves
in God, placing all their trust

So, on this day we gather
rejoicing as we still strive
and remember that our TRUE celebration
was June 19, 1865

The day WE were emancipated from slavery
formally with a decree
the day our people gained THEIR independence
the day WE were originally set free.

Happy Valentine's Day To The Lonely Heart

Valentine's Day can be depressing
when you have no one to share,
no one to send you flowers
or just plain blank be there
We, the ones without
tend to hate this holiday,
we try to omit the hours
not like some who try to delay
We stay in our shelter
maybe an old love will call,
but we find out later
it was a waste of time, that's all
Us in whom are blessed with children
focus this day only on them
but deep inside there's a yearning
for that special him
So, to my lonely hearts out there
for every one, there are five,
kiss your children, enjoy the day
and thank the Lord to be alive
There is someone out there for you
you may not meet him right away,
there is a next year to find
a special someone to celebrate this day
Keep the faith, hold your head up
smile, God makes a way
enjoy the moment, seize the challenge
and have a blessed Valentine's Day.

It Isn't Fair

I don't think it's fair
I don't think it's right
on Mother's Day, you wear red
but my carnation is white

When you want to see her
you don't have to imagine her face
but me, I have to visit
that cemetery place

If you get lonely
and feeling despair
you can pick up the phone
your mother is there

For me, it's quite different
I cry, I sob, I brawl
although I speak
there is no one at all

There are some who are blessed
but they disrespect, yell and curse
while my mother's last ride
was in the back of a hearse

They take advantage of the woman
who raised them to be
I even heard some wish
that they were me

But little do they know
a treasure I would give
if for five minutes of time
for my mother to live

If you are one of those
you need to recognize
the future is unpredictable
no one knows where it lies

I've been through that scene
riding in that long Cadillac
your feelings are distraught
I would never go back

So, on this Mother's Day
take the time to share
give your mom a kiss and a hug
because I tell you, it isn't fair.

It's Not About Us

Christmas may make you feel emotional
this may be true
but please keep in mind
it's not about me, nor about you

It's not about presents
or the gifts you may acquire
it's not about a decorated tree
it's way much higher

It's not about ribbons,
boxes and bows
it's not about lights,
Santa or mistletoes

But it's about a man
who came to earth
who saw our hearts
and he knew our worth

Who took 33 years
of torture and pain
just for us
with no earthly reward to gain

Who hung, bled and died
on the rugged old cross
to save all of us
He knew we'd be lost

A man so great
with wisdom and power
He gets the glory
every day, every hour

So, when Christmas Day comes
and presents you see
remember that it's about Him
a man who set you free

A man who loves you
more and more
with each passing day
more than before

The Alpha, The Omega
The Holy One, The Lamb
this man is Jesus
The Great I Am

LET'S TALK ABOUT LOVE

How can you talk about love
and not mention God's name?
For his love is the greatest
and always remains the same

He so loved the world
he gave his only son
so that we might love one another
and get his work on earth done

He loves you so much
for you, he took the time to create
special, down to the detail
He did not imitate

He knows all about you
your faults, your fears, your cares
He even knows
the number of your hairs

Who but your father
who has all the power
could love you so great
even in your darkest hour?

Regardless of the trials
or tribulations you don't understand
just know he's holding you
in the palm of his hand

No love I know greater
no sweeter debt that I owe
than to carry his love
and peace, that I know

He fills us up
with his love by and by
know that you are loved
by your father, The Most High

With him, there's no day set aside
every day is the same
let's talk about love
and God is his name

Motherless To Motherless

I want you to know
that I understand how you feel
your heart is breaking
and the pain you feel is real
My mother has been gone
twenty-three years to date
so on Mother's Day I get depressed
this holiday, I hate
But God blessed me with children
on whom I can love and care
I see my mother in their eyes
so I know she is always there
I'm not going to tell you
that the pain will go away
all these years have gone by
but it feels like yesterday
She will live forever
because she's embedded in your heart
the memories of her will comfort you
for the time that you're apart
Nothing is promised to us
not even today or tomorrow
so seize the time that you have
and put away your sorrow
Ask yourself this question:
Is sad what my mother would want me to be?
Or would she want me to celebrate
with my children and be happy?

Your mother is not gone
she just went to a better place
that palace in the clouds
and to sing 'Amazing Grace'
I know you miss your mother
because I feel the same way too
but she's everywhere you go
to aid and watch over you.

MOTHER'S DAY POEM TO MY CHILDREN

Although I might not say it
as often as I should
if I could give you the world
believe me, I would

There were times when I got angry,
there were times when I felt blue,
but as long as the sun may shine
so will my love for you

Eighteen years is a long time
from beginning to end,
from scraped-up knees to broken hearts
nothing that time wouldn't mend

I'll hold you in my arms
I will rock you to sleep
and in my heart forever
you all, I will always keep

So, children, keep in mind
although there may be others
there is no special or greater love
than the one of your mother's.

My Father, My Friend

I have a father
who means my life to me
so much more
than one may see

He gives me love
and so much more
and with each new day
it is more than before

He's always there
no matter what comes my way
He guides me when
I am confused or led astray

He comforts me
in the times that I need
and holds me close
when my heart bleed

He is my father
and also my friend
He promises to be with me
until the end

I can go to him
when I am lost or sad
I can count on him
to make me glad

So, on this Father's Day
as you rejoice in love
I too will rejoice
for my father up above.

Now We Are As One

I never thought I'd feel
as I do today,
there once was a time
when my skies were grey

But we both crossed paths
and our love was meant to be,
this love that we share
will last an eternity

My better half, my partner,
the love of my life
our days to come will be sweet
as we live as man and wife

I'll promise you the moon
and we'll both have the sun,
our love is our destiny
now we are as one.

SPECIAL MOTHER'S DAY TRIBUTE

Today marks a special day
to celebrate our mother
a woman who birthed us
to each, there is no other

But I would like to thank today
a woman so humble and pure
the faith she carried within her
through all she had to endure

Her obedience was evidence
of the God-fearing woman she was
so meek and well-blessed
a loving heart, just because

She was chosen by God
to carry his only son
God knew all about her
and that she would get his work done

A woman without sinful compromise
the birth mother of The Great I Am
The Holy One, The Only One
The Messiah, Lord of Lords, The Lamb

Thank you, Mary, for your faithfulness
and being obedient to your call
for the birth of our Savior
who in turn, saved us all

So, on this special day
I salute and commend you
the birth mother of our Lord and Savior
giving honor that's over due.

THE GREAT I AM

Today we celebrate life
and not just any one
we celebrate his life
that was given by God's son

Every lash that he took
he took it for you and I
not one word did he mumble
he didn't even sigh

He suffered in silence
the love for us was so great
he wanted to save us
he wanted to change our fate

This day is not about a dress
a suit, a tie, where you dine
but it's about the bread of life
the good shepherd, the true vine

A man who laid down his life
sacrificed and died
in three days he arose
a man to be praised and glorified

Through him we are saved
covered by the blood that he shed
the gift to be free
and comfort from words he said

You see, today is not about a bunny
it is about a lamb
who was wounded for our transgressions
Jesus…the great I AM!

THE MAN FROM GALILEE

The man from Galilee
who unselfishly gave his life for you and me
so that this world can be free
oh, bless that man from Galilee

Although the bunny is funny
and the colored eggs are great
but it was the divine purpose of Jesus
why we truly celebrate

Jesus' purpose was to come
and to save all who were lost
despised and rejected
they nailed him to the cross

They called him names and laughed,
'Jesus of Nazareth, you say…
if that's true, son of God,
then save yourself today.'

Not one word did he mumble
but as his journey came to an end
fulfillment of his purpose
to save the world from sin

Darkness filled the sky
the people out of fear cried
for now, some realized
who they actually crucified

Still with unbelief
him, these people continued to mock
as they placed him in a tomb
and covered the doorway with a rock

Laughter continued to echo throughout
as they believed he was dead
they desecrated his burial
marking "King of the Jews" over his head

But on the third day
when Mary came to see
the cloth folded neatly in his place
and the tomb was empty

He is not here
all you will find are his clothes
with all power in his hand
just like he said, he arose

Praise be to God
who hung, bled and died for you and me
who rose on the third day with all power
Jesus Christ, the man from Galilee.

Dedication Pieces

A Blessed Birthday

F is for the fun we had, the days we spent together
R is for memories we share that will last forever
I is for the incentive you gave whenever I lost my way
E is for the encouragement you passed when I went astray
N is for a nimbus over your head which only angels wear
D is for the dreams that we dream that only friends share

Some people come into our lives for different reasons
temporary, permanent or just for a season
I cherish our friendship from the day we met
our fond memories I will never forget
Special is what you are to me in every way
that is why I'm wishing you a blessed birthday.

A Blessing In Disguise

I never knew your love was so strong
until I looked into your eyes,
I never knew you cared so much…
a love in disguise.
You raised me from a child to an adult
wiped my tears away,
you comforted me with your kindness
and showed me a brighter day.
You laughed at my subtle jokes
and made me realize,
that I too am truly loved…
a blessing in disguise.
What makes a person so special
is the way they are inside,
a heart so big and made of gold
and arms held out open wide.
I thank the heavenly father up above
for the closeness of our ties,
He blessed me with a special aunt…
my blessing in disguise.

<u>A Child Care Provider's Prayer</u>

Lord, as each day begins,
let me begin it with you
knowing, no matter what comes,
you will see me through

As I prepare for my job,
I know you will meet me there
to use me to mold your children
as I provide child care

Please bless my vision
so I can see through their little eyes
the innocence, the yearning
or what hurt tries to disguise

Bless my hands so I can be
a comfort or I can mend
to wipe a tear if need be,
to be the loving hands you send

Touch my mind please, Father
so I will have thoughts of you and not man
to give of myself
and try to understand

Please bless my ears
so more than just words I can hear
to assure to the children
I am listening and I am near

Bless my heart, Oh God,
to love with all that I have to give
to go beyond measure
and to teach them to live

Remind me to be humble
and remember I too was once young
and someone was there to guide me
as my life begun

With patience, understanding
and all the love I hold within
ready to shape and mold a child
as their day begins

Keep your arms around the children, Lord,
and bless them all the same
may they see a bit of you in me…
this is my prayer, in Jesus' name.

A Mother

To my darling children…

A mother is someone who is always there
someone who understands the burdens you bear
Someone who not only bandages your knee
but kisses the booboo away and set the pain free
Someone who understands your talk
holds your hand as you prepare to walk
Stay up late to make sure the homework is done
and please don't forget the errands they run
Wipe the tears with the words they choose
helps you learn to tie your shoes
A doctor, lawyer, cook, a seamstress to mend
a mother's job never ends
A mother can also be a friend too
and that is what I was to all of you.

Love always and definitely forever,
Your Mother.

A Mother, A Sister, A Friend

A virtuous woman is what I see
when I look upon your face
a woman holding up her family
who has dignity and grace

Someone that I can talk to
I can relax and just be me
someone I can laugh with
and remain worry-free

I'm thankful for you are a part of my life
you've taught me so very much
I've watched you spread your love
and use your motherly touch

You accepted me as I am
with love, our relationship grew
and if I ever needed anything
I know I can depend on you

God-sent, you are to me
until the very end
you are a dear mother, a sister
and most importantly, a friend.

Admiration

Although I've only known you
for just a little while
I've grown to understand
while in pain, that you do smile

I've learned that you are determined
strongminded and have strong will,
you have an appointed destination
and a goal you must fulfill

Highly intelligent and educated black woman
strong but yet inside, still a girl,
giving your all every day
and taking on the world

Bearing it's weight on your shoulder
struggling hard, paving your way,
I look up to you in admiration
and hope to be just as strong one day.

God's Gift

I went to the drug store today
to pick out a card
although each one was touching
picking one was very hard
I wanted one to tell you
how appreciative that I am
that you stood by my side
when I got myself in a jam
I wanted one to say
how much of a friend you have been
one that I can confide in
from beginning to end
I wanted one to inform you
that you are one of a kind
with a special gift
which is hard to find
There was a logical reason
why at first we met
a reason we may never understand
but will never forget
It was as if our lives were destined
we were meant to be
you searching for fulfillment
and me, a family
God ran our lives through
so that our paths would cross
He knew that you would guide me
for I was definitely lost

He knew there would be an attachment
a bond like no other
for love knows no boundaries
there were none between each other
I cannot thank him enough
for this gift he gave to me
when I went to him in prayer
He said it was a lifetime guarantee
I'm glad you are in my life
for you are truly God-sent
our friendship I will forever treasure
because it is my best present.

Happy Birthday, Aunt Hilda

There's not enough paper in this world
to write how I feel about you
to show you how much you mean to me
and to tell you how I'm grateful for all you do.

You have been a blessing in so many ways
you have been by my side through thick and thin,
when I thought I had almost lost and gave up,
you still encouraged me to win.

You supported my dreams and rubbed my head
you comforted me while I was blue,
you enlightened my path and redirected me,
I'm blessed because I have you.

The promise you made to my mom
did not include the grown-up years,
but you still make sure I have, me and my kids
you console me with my fears.

As I write this poem, trying not to cry
because I know without you I'd be lost,
you have been, and continue to be
my comforter, no matter the cost.

So, on this 70th birthday of yours
I wish you peace and love,
You're more than just an aunt to me
You're an aunt beyond comparison, a gift from above.
I Love You, Aunt Hilda

My Gifts

Just once I'd like to have
A whole world of my own
Share it with someone
Have to watch it get full grown
Everyone needs someone
Many have sought this to be true
All my dreams have become reality
Lost love, I've found and it's you
I never thought I could love anyone
As much as I love you
Having you in my life has brought great joy
Joy through and through
An angel sent from heaven above
Making my dreams exclaim
Each one of you are a blessing from God
Sweethearts of mine: Ja She', Maliah and James.

Poem For Barbara

This too shall pass
although at times it feels quite numbing
you have to go through it to get to it
but your better day is coming

I know some days you feel lost
please know you're not alone
if we could, we'd share your burden
so you wouldn't bear this on your own

The days ahead may not be easy
but take one day at its best
smell the flowers, take a walk
and give your a body and soul a rest

No need to worry about tomorrow
God has it all in his hands
your name, situation, doubts and fears
and you, he understands

This is just a process
there's no testimony without a test
you are more than a conqueror
be patient, his glory will manifest

The hardest thing to do is wait
this I know to be true
but wait and be of good courage
God will see you through

He went ahead of you
to make the crooked places straight
just adhere to his voice and follow him
and on him, patiently wait

Another chapter in your book
filled with God's grace, mercy and his loving kiss
trusting, praying, believing and knowing
through Him, you got this!

SISTERLY LOVE

We've been through a lot
a lot of good times and bad
we've made each other happy
we've made each other mad

But through it all
our love stood strong
the kind of love
that can't go wrong

A sister's love
is a bonded one, I'm told
it's the kind of love
that lasts until you're old

I've never believed
this myth to be true
until that very day
that I knew you

You've been by my side
through thick and through thin
you helped me out
when all my out was in

You've wiped my tears
with the words that you said
you've given me advice
when I was misled

A true friend indeed
over the years, you've became
two different people
but the love is still the same

All the love that I give
all the love that you gave
will forever exist
from cradle to grave.

Soul of A Typesetter

I sit at my computer
and I type obituaries every day
I see people come and go
and some, I made a friend along the way.
As I scan their picture image,
my heart pounds, my blood race,
then their picture is on the screen
it hurts to see their face.
It pains me to have to type
an obituary with a friend's name,
knowing this is their last farewell
and their families won't be the same.
My job gets very complicated
as I turn their whole life into a book,
all those years of living
and one day, their breath was took.
With every letter that I type
a piece of me is in it's place
but comforted to know
one day I will see their face.
All different ages
but they are very dear to me,
no more pain, no more sorrow
they are finally free.

The Trial of A Mother

Days, weeks, months, years seem to fly by
with each day passing, I try and I try
I try to be a good mother and show you the right way
but from me, your mother, you did go astray
I understand sometimes you'd like to be left alone
but there is a difference between being and acting grown
Making your own decisions takes maturity and trust
you have to remember you can't be unjust
I try to encourage you to be the best that you can
be your own person and have no dependencies on man
But you seem to follow down a treacherous road
not capable of handling its heavy load
How am I supposed to react to this rebellious teen?
Who thinks the streets are safe but her mother is mean?
Should I let her go or put her on lock and key?
wanting her to succeed and have a better life than me
I'm torn between this, but then again, I'm not
it's like the question is, "a warm bed or a cold cot?"
Being a teen can be hard; still young, yet grown
wanting to be independent but can't make it on your own
Warm bed or a cold cot? I'd choose the warm bed
that way I know I'll have somewhere to lay my head
But this rebellious teen is stubborn too,
so what do you think a good mother would do?
I'm baffled by this but I'd be hurt if she were gone
so, like a good mother, I'll just hold on.

To A Friend

A friend is someone so close and so dear
a person who knows your dreams and fears
A physical companion with whom you spiritually connect
who understands you and puts things into prospect
A person by your side whether you're wrong or right
who listens to you cry, comforting you day or night
A person so God-sent with love unconditional and true
who believes in you even when you don't believe in you
A person with advice when you're feeling deterred
there's even closeness when there are no words
One is blessed when they find such a friend
someone they can lean on or have a hand to extend
Their life can be changed with their kind word or thought
their emotional and mental battles would be easier fought
These things I have said I know to be true
for I have found a friend like that, and that friend is you.

To My Aunt, With Love

There aren't any words
that can truly express what you mean to me
you've raised me from a child
and I know it wasn't easy.
You gave me everything
that a child could want and more
you put the wind beneath my wings
so that I could take off and soar
I'm forever grateful
for this sacrifice you gave
my love for you is deeply embedded
and in my heart, it will be saved
You've taken the role to me as mother
you've lived up to that name,
you have taught me love and respect
and helped me be the woman I became
I'm sure my mother would be proud
of the job you did while she was gone,
that is why she left me in your care
so that my life would go on
A Nana to my children
a mother you are to me
heaven-sent to all of us
and very blessed are we.

To My Friend

If ever a friend had to prove their loyalty
that is what you have done to me

You went through great lengths to get me by
not once did you grumble, nor said, "I'll try"

You suffered in silence and yet with a smile
you knew in your heart that
true friendships are worthwhile

I hope you will call me if you're ever in a spot
and trust that I will give it all that I got

Because that is what you have definitely done
you're greatly appreciated and compared to none

I'm taking this time out to thank you with a pen,
thank you for loving me so much
and thanks for being my friend.

TO MY HUSBAND ON OUR ANNIVERSARY

I can recall when we first met
circumstances would not allow,
but because of all we've been through
our love is much stronger now

I had no idea a difference you'd make
to me in my own world,
you have changed and filled me so
from where I came; a little girl

How can someone love another
without losing a grip on self,
but you've proved that and more
without me being placed on a shelf

You filled a void in my life
one in which I had no clue,
you satisfied a warming desire
I am complete because of you

As we face the challenges of this world
united together we will stand,
we'll walk side by side
and keep our hands in God's hand

On this special day, I give to you
all of me, my entire life,
accepting you as my husband
and me, being your loving wife

I love you with all my heart
let no doubt enter, it is true
I'm so glad our paths have crossed
and I am glad that I found you.

Happy Anniversary

TO MY SON ON HIS BIRTHDAY

Happy birthday little one
may your day be special and bright
and may all your dreams be sweet
as I kiss you goodnight

May you never have to struggle
work hard and you will achieve
never settle for less
and always believe

Believe in yourself, trust in the Lord
He will always be by your side
if your way becomes unclear
He will be your guide

Listen to your heart
you won't go wrong, you'll see
and know you'll be the man
I've raised you to be

Respect your elders
don't drink, don't smoke, don't curse
don't steal because crime pays
put God in your life first

The road that you'll travel
won't be easy but you try
giving up is a scapegoat
yes, real men do cry

You can't get something for nothing
the world is give and take
just don't take more than you give
because you lay in the bed you make

Sorry to babble on
but for you I want the best
I know with my encouragement
your life will manifest

So, my baby boy, Tre' James
whatever come what may
I hope all your dreams come true
make a wish, Happy Birthday!

What If

I know you've heard the cliché
'more excuses than a man going to jail'
but what about…
'more excuses than a man going to hell?'

What if God made excuses
the same that you fail
What then would you do?
What would your life tell?

What if He said 'Sorry,
but I was doing what I do…
you know how it is,
sorry I could not heal you.'

My bad, my child,
I didn't feel like it at the time
I was tired, just got in
all those hills to climb

I know you called me
yes, I ignored my phone
I was having a pity party
and wanted to be alone

What if God did that to us?
Make excuses like we do?
What if he took a break
only because he wanted to?

What if He said to us
'I have too much on my plate
so whatever your need is,
your need is going to have to wait'

I can't worship today
I'm tired, it's too far
but yet still, he blessed you
with that brand new car

What if God did that to us?
Make excuses like we do?
Thank you, Lord, for not being like us
But continue to see us through.

Other Poems

A Bus Driver's Prayer

Lord, I come to you
knee bow and bent before your grace
asking that you bless this bus
and safely take us to our place

Bless my hands for they steer
keep us safely on the road
bless my feet, for they use the brakes
I'm carrying a precious load

Keep my mind focused
and please allow me to stay alert
for deeply in my heart
not one of your children I want to hurt

Send your anointing please, Father
keep us closely in your care
you promised in your word
that you would always be there

Thank you, Lord, for it now
your traveling angels, I know you'll send
in Jesus' name I pray to you
thankfully I say, Amen.

AM I MY BROTHER'S KEEPER?

Am I my brother's keeper?
That's a question to ask yourself
Do I listen when they need to talk?
Or do I put them on a shelf?

Do I respond when they reach out?
Do I answer when they call?
Am I the family I'm supposed to be
when their back is against the wall?

Am I my brother's keeper?
Will I push them away because of time?
I'm too busy, I'll call later,
they're okay, they'll be fine

Am I my brother's keeper?
Do I truly love my family in Christ?
Or are they people I just see
on Sunday and bible study night?

Am I my brother's keeper?
Do I even know what it mean?
To stand firm and hold someone up
and allow them to lean.

Am I my brother's keeper?
Do I put myself aside-
and lend a shoulder or two,
be the one in whom they can confide?

Am I my brother's keeper?
The true answer lies within you,
all that you say
and most definitely all that you do

Am I my brother's keeper?
Or do my church family go on a shelf?
A Sunday, bible study night family
that's what you need to ask yourself

Look into your heart…
are you just a sweeper?
Sweeping your family under the rug
or are you your brother's keeper?

Born Again

Born from your mother's womb
into a life of sin
but to enter the Kingdom of God
you must be born again

Baptized in the river of Jordan
Jesus paved the way
to do his father's will
and to save us today

You must confess all of your sins
and give all of your heart
and baptism plays a role
where your sins from you can depart

For God so loved the world
he gave his only begotten son
that we will follow his path
and get his work done

Praise his holy name
for he is coming again
repent and be baptized
to wash away your sin

One thing that God asks of you
is that you give in to his grace
in exchange for eternal life
and to see his face

Born from your mother's womb
into a life of sin
you can see the Kingdom of God
if you are born again.

FAMILY

F is for the foundation that my ancestors started
A is for all of our members who were dearly departed
M is for my mother who passed her name to me
I is for the independent woman I came to be
L is for the love that we share through and through
Y is for YOU because you are part of my family too.

Freedom

Free is a small four-letter word that's often been abused
some folks take it for granted and tend to misuse
There are different types of free
and here are some which appeal to me
There is freedom from jail, no bars hold you down
the solitary life, no way to get around
Right to vote, right to speak
a freedom mostly misused by the illiterate and weak
Then there is freedom of alcohol and illegal drugs
that should be replaced with kisses and hugs
But the best freedom I love is the privilege just to be free
to be who I am, to stand up and just be me.

GRANDMA'S WORDS

Back in the good ole' days
Grandma used to say,
"Go to sleep now, my children,
for tomorrow, we must go to church and pray."

We'd get up Sunday morning
rise and shine, breakfast done
get dressed for Sunday school
time to learn, no time for fun

But over the years
Satan's influence became stronger and stronger
he'll catch your child's attention
and hold it longer and longer

Grandma knew what she was doing
she knew the devil would have our souls
so we knelt right beside her
and did as we were told

Grandma always told us
pray every day and every night
push away temptation
God will make it all right

Grandma is no longer with us
but her words in my head still stand
I now take my children to church
so the devil can't get their hand.

I Am A Writer

There are some people who can dance
some who can sing and some that write
I am a writer
I don't sleep at night
I lay in my bed trying to get a good night
but as my eyes close, my brain starts to recite
I jump to the floor and turn on the light
grab a notebook and pen and I begin to write.

I write about feelings, traumas and tales
I write about life and men in jail
I'm not Langston Hughes or Gwendolyn Brooks
I just write how I feel in one of my notebooks
I am a writer
I love to write
If the notion strikes me
I'll write all night
because…I am a writer.

I'M NOT TIRED

I have a million and one things to do today
I have to see my boss, I have to get my papers straight,
I'm not tired.

No, I didn't get much sleep last night
after working five until ten plus finishing my homework
Coffee? No thank you,
I said I'm not tired.

Everyone is depending on me
to handle certain situations and get the job done
No, I can't take a break. Vacation has to wait.
I'm not tired.

Appointments, bills, students, faculty, kids, husband!!
I wish there were more than just one of me
because boy, being pulled from
fifteen different directions will wear you out!
Let me just rest for a minute.
Whew!

Ten years later…

Wow! I feel great!
I must have been tired.

In His Name

You are made in his image
to be like Christ
saved by grace
and brought with a price

Born to serve and worship
acknowledging him in all you do
letting him order your steps
he will see you through

But sin crept in
and took over, and YOU, it consumed
filling you up
with darkness and gloom

Now it doesn't seem clear
there's confusion and pain
your living became lost
and somewhat in vain

But there is a man
who can wash you clean
regardless of the situation
he knows the unseen

Just let him come in
and fill you to the rim
he can create in you anew
if you just trust in him

Once in his presence
you'll never be the same
he will shape you and mold you
and JESUS is his name!

Jesus, My All In All

Hello, my friend.
How is your life? Is Jesus in it?
Since God has entered my life, I find myself not worrying over stuff that I used to worry over. I realize that he will take care of me and that no matter how much I had worried in the past, he was still in control. I realized that even in the midst of pain, I can still call on Jesus' name and he will hear my humble cry. I realized that without him I am nothing and through him I can do anything. I find comfort, strength and peace in knowing that he is my savior and redeemer. I am so glad and overjoyed that I found Jesus but also relieved that he never lost me. I don't know where I'd be without him today.
I praise him when I am happy. I praise him when I am sad. He is my doctor, lawyer, mother, father, sister, brother and friend. He is my all in all. I love Jesus with all of my heart and soul. I know that he was sent here on earth to be my savior. I know that he died on the cross on calvary for my sins so that I can have everlasting life. I know that he loves me, for he stretched out his arms and died for me. By his grace and mercy, I still live and breathe.
I thank the Lord for all he has done for me, for what he is doing right now and for what he is going to do. He is my provider and my comforter in times of distress. Jesus is love. He loves us all and has a plan for each of us. He just wants us to obey his commandments and treat each other with love and respect. My heavenly father is awaiting for me in his sanctuary and when the old world is over and gone, my new home will be with the Lord, resting in his bosom forever. Amen.

Little Sheep Lost

Little sheep lost who went astray
who got confused and lost their way
blinded by sin and didn't realize
it was a wolf in a sheep's disguise
How can I get back and hear my master's voice?
But this was my mess, I made this choice
Just like a true master, he will find his lost sheep
because the soul, he wants to keep
scared to return because of the stray
I will be punished and put away
but the master is gentle, he loves me more
I yearn even more than before
He will find me although this sin I am in
and he will clean me and make me whole again
because my master, he paid the cost
for all of the sins and his little sheep lost.

Long Lost Love

A teenage love is what we shared
we were young and lost into each other
then life took a turn, you moved away
we both then found a significant other

We lived our lives far apart
you with yours and me with mine
never knowing what life had in store
or down the road, what we would find

We each suffered a great deal
from the loss of our mates
both hearts broken from all the pain
for it to end, we could not wait

Time passed on as it always does
a turn took place in our lives once more
the first love that we both once knew so well
was back just as it was before

Because of a twist of fate
a love connection happened like no other
you found me and I found you
once again, we're lost into each other.

Mrs. C

Mrs. C...she think she got me
but she is unaware
of who I am
or the fruit I bear

For through the eyes of God, the Creator
the beginning and the end
I can do all things through Christ
my broken heart, he will mend

I am conformed from his image
it's me he covers and protects
the enemy may try to overtake me
but in my life, she is a reject

Mrs. C...the immortal enemy think she's got me
she's unaware of the fruit I bear
not knowing wherever I go
God will meet me there

I am the salt of the earth
I am part of the True Vine
I am more than a conqueror
and through him I am refined

I have peace and been justified
and I know who my savior is
I am God's gift to Christ
yes, I am one of His

Mrs. C thinks she knows about me
she believes that I am weak
but God gives me strength every day
therefore, I am strong and I am meek

No weapon formed against me shall prosper
no pestilence, no disease
on my knees I will fight her
my heart and mind is at ease

Right now I may be going through the fire
but there won't be any soot on me
this is just a test for my testimony
time to go for blows with Mrs. C

She can't move my faith, blurr my vision
or cause my light to dim
for he is my healer, my redeemer
and I am holding on to his garments' hem

I have the power to speak over my life
and I choose to live and not die
So, Mrs. C, from you I am free
I declare this in the name of Jesus,
you're not wanted… Goodbye!

<u>My Prayer</u>

I said a prayer last night. I didn't say it very loud, nor did I say it in front of people. I didn't say it on my knees, nor did I fold my hands. But, I knew that he heard every word that I said. It wasn't very long, nor did I repent. Although I started to cry, I knew he still understood what I said.

I said a prayer last night and I know God heard every word that I said. Some people tend to forget the little things that God does but I don't. He woke me up this morning started me on my way. He put me in my right mind and helped me begin my day. He knows just what I need and all my needs he will supply. He's my friend indeed and comforts me when I cry. I go to him when I'm confused, I go to him when I'm down, I know I can count on him because he's always around. God so loved the world that he gave his only begotten son. My trust I put in him completely because like him, there is no other one. If you hold on and keep your faith, no matter if things seem untrue, believe me, he will be there to hold and comfort you. I said a prayer for you today.

NIGHT SHIFT

Some say that a lot of people struggle with sleep
because sleep requires peace
calmness…freedom from disturbance
where there is no war, or a war has ceased

Their frame of mind is cluttered
with the day's struggles, aches and pains
so there is no tranquility
and the struggles still remains

The tossing and the turning
in the middle of the night
their flesh and their spirit
raging in a fight

God said in his Word, don't worry about anything
instead, pray about everything in the name of his son
tell him what you need
and thank him for all that he has done

Then you will experience God's peace
which exceeds more than we can understand
his peace will guard our hearts and minds in Jesus
as we trust and learn to put it all in his hands

Do you have God's peace
embedded within your heart?
Can your faith sustain through the winds
when your life is blowing apart?

It's time to be at peace
having faith and knowing God will see us through
night is for resting, not wrestling
knowing God works the night shift, not you!

No Excuse

The feast is prepared, the table is set
the invitation has been sent to all able
come, for everything is now ready
to sit at the master's table

Every Sunday morning, God prepares a feast
it's your choice if you'll be there
your gift which was given to you
is part of that feast for you to share

God blessed you with a gift
but it is not yours to keep
it is for you to bless someone else
for what you sow, you shall reap

There is not one excuse
to the invitation that you deny
sitting on your gift from God
it's like saying, 'I won't comply"

The table is set, your gift is part of the feast
but the choice is yours; put your gift to use
no matter the reason that may arise
there really is no excuse.

PLEASE BE KIND

Wounded and pain-ravaged people are all around us
some suffering in silence, some acting it out
holding back tears while grieving, worried or fearful
yet inside, the emptiness loudly shouts

There are some whose children are terminally ill
families with no idea how to keep on the lights
kids being bullied in their school
some wanting to end their life because they don't feel right

There are couples in the middle of a messy divorce
people grieving over a loved one or ended relationship
spouses whose partners are deployed in combat
and single parents with little help and need just a grip

Everyone has their own story
yet none has a sign saying, 'I'm struggling. Be nice to me."
and since they don't, we need to look more closely
look more deeper into what we see

We must allow God to use us, to spread his love
don't speak, but think first and not let your words condemn
but let him give you the words to speak
so through you, they can see and feel him

Everyone one of us are delicate, a vulnerable treasure
we all need to be handled with care
we all need to love and feel we're loved
and reassured that God will hear us and be there

So, as you make your way through today
people won't alert you that they're struggling or a
broadcast you won't find,
but if you look with the right eyes, you'll see the signs
proceed with caution and remember, please be kind.

Portrait of A Soul

Here I am in a facility
with no other place to go
a different type of lifestyle
with none of the things I know

I used to drive my Lexus
staring out the window and see
the envy of all types of people
being jealous of me

Walking into my townhouse
petting my poodle on the head
Nicole, the maid, cooking dinner
Joe, the butler, turning down my bed

I loved the life I had
to need and want, we didn't know
my husband, the doctor, two fine kids
our seeds, we did sow

We ate at the finest restaurants
we drank expensive wine
spur of the moment Mexico trips
on a cruise, ourselves we'd find

We did not mingle with such
Blacks, Hispanics and Jews
our belief would not allow it
we'd spit on them if we choose

They were only good for one thing
and that was to serve us
in my opinion, I think
they didn't deserve the back of the bus

Now the children are grown
they eventually left the house
my husband turned to another woman
he is no longer my spouse

I suffered a nervous breakdown
my stroke messed up my right side and one eye
the wheelchair that I use
it sort of gets me by

The prejudice life that I lived
seemed to have taken its toll
for now, these are the people I depend on
for I am confined and I am old

I have no control in my life
the same people that I hated so much
are the same ones who take care of me
with such a loving touch

And here I am in a facility
to go back and change things, I would give
I'm fighting mind, body and soul
every day just to live.

Remember When

Remember when our nights were long
and our days were fun
we took cozy walks
in the mid-evening sun?

Remember when we sat alone
and the sky was blue?
We whispered sweet nothings
and I love you's

Remember when
you held me tight
in the midst of rain
and in the warm moonlight?

Remember when
we shared our dreams?
But problems arose
they were ripped at the seams

Remember when
the sky went grey?
Now all we share
is a rainy day

All the times we shared
if you want it just like then
just close your eyes
and just…remember when.

Senior

I carry the memories
from one generation to the next
I've been through hard times
the times that were perplex

I am the mother
of all mothers to be
the very top limb
of the family tree

I've been blessed
to have seen many a day
my hand in God's hand
every step of the way

Over the years
I've gained knowledge galore
I've given of myself
until I was rundown and tore

I'm more advanced
in dignity and rank
you may have seen the movie
but I've witnessed the ship that sank

I've earned my respect
by being the mentor and elder
I am the beginning
for I am a Senior.

The Depression

How can I be happy
when I am feeling such pain and misery?
My heart aches all the time
because of agony

Although my soul is crying
I still wear a smile on my face
but when the lights go off
I feel so out of place

Some days I feel like screaming
I feel like shouting or just die
but once again
I hold it in and all I do is cry

I don't know why my heart is in pain
why the grief torments me so
I wish I knew so I could help
by just letting the problem go

Maybe it's not really something
What else could it be?
Maybe it's not anyone
maybe it's just me.

THE GHOST THAT TAUNT ME

There is a scary feeling which taunts me
a feeling that worries me the most
I'm conquering this scary feeling every day
this feeling that I named 'Ghost'

There are many ghosts in my head
from the past up until this day
they speak to me every now and then
which redirects my way

These ghosts remind me all the time
of all the mistakes I have made
all the misery and pain I've suffered
as if away they never fade

They intervene in my everyday life
and distract me from my goal
they hold me down from moving on
and rip at my vulnerable soul

But there is one way I can overcome
these taunting ghosts which grieve
if I hold up my head, live for the future
and if…I believe.

The Race

Growing up I was always told
that things change as you get old,
the life you lived reflects on you
it shows all of what you've been through

My grandmother says, 'Back in the day,
the human race were gone astray…
our lives were divided because of skin,
brown was *out* and white was *in*'

Racial tension grew so much in time
we struggle to save a penny and dime,
Martin Luther King knew there would be
a better day for you and me

As I grew older I realized
that it's still there, it's just disguised
prejudice is nationally felt
enough so, to make your heart melt

But more and more, day by day
I'm trying to make a better way
to deal with the racial tension I see
maybe not for them, but within me.

Too Late

"Oh, Lord, have mercy on my soul"
I said as I approached the gates of heaven
I have known of the Lord
ever since the age of seven.
Soon, a man met me at the gate
and said, "Dear child, I'm sorry to say
that this is as far as you can go
because from God, you did go astray.
You did not seek him faithfully
and his commandments, you disobeyed,
you didn't even take the time
to humble yourself and pray.
You thought you were living right
because you didn't drink or swear,
not one time did you acknowledge him
nor for this day did you prepare."

I pleaded with this man saying,
"I'm begging for forgiveness now,
there must be something I can do
to get in the gate somehow."
He raised up his brow
and soon began to pace
when he looked back up at me
a tear rolled down his face.
"How can I say this gently?" he said
"and so that you may understand?
Your praises unto the Lord
were very few and quite bland."

"You called on him once or twice
but only because of sickness and pain,
the life you led was without him
so your living became in vain.
You went to church only on Easter
and then it was only to impress,
you wanted everyone to take notice
of your expensive new dress.
When he spoke to your heart
and tried to get you to acknowledge him,
you turned your back and failed to listen
and Jesus, you then condemned."

"There is no way I can let you by,
you should have pleaded to him before,
you now must depart from this gate
and be banned forever more.
I'm sorry my child, but it has to be
there's no one to blame, you caused your fate,
now you know what was asked of you
but I'm afraid it is now too late."

What's In A Name

All because of a rumor
all because a lie was told
the name that I now have
is the name I will forever hold
I guess she must have thought
he would be a man like he's suppose
but all it was, was just a thought
for no one ever knows
My roots were all mistaken
the life I led was a deception
the life I lived, the love I gave
was a mere lie from conception
I am so confused
because of this lie my mother began
daddy couldn't explain it
I guess no one can
On my paper of birth under "Father"
his name is written in black and white
he had to have signed the bottom
but yet and still knew it wasn't right
By doing so, he acknowledged the fact
that his daughter am I
he knew at that very moment
my life was going to be a lie
I'm baffled by this decision
my so-called parents came to pass
it seems as if it was just a joke
and they both had a laugh

Did they think I wouldn't know?
Or how my future would turn?
Would I be hurt
over this lie that I learn?
They were not thinking
when to me, they pulled a prank
for all that it mattered
she could have left it blank
Although my mother is gone
I still carry his name
it doesn't really matter
because I am me just the same.

When My Time Is Up

When my time is up
let my life not be in vain
let his doors swing wide open
as I call on Jesus' name

Let God greet me at the gate
saying, "My child, well done.
You have done your work on earth
and prayed in the name of my son."

May I have taught all there is to teach
and learned all there is to learn
may a seat in His Kingdom
be what I have earned

My loved ones will be saddened
but it's not for very long
for soon they will realize
with God is where I belong

May I be blessed with his fulfillment
which overruns my cup
may I be all he wants me to be
when my time is up.

To my sister, La Keisha. From cradle to grave, I love you to the moon and back mama. Love, Muskiletta

www.ingramcontent.com/pod-product-compliance
Lightning Source LLC
Chambersburg PA
CBHW060355080526
44583CB00012B/331